The Allergy-Free Vegetarian Cookbook

OTHER BOOKS BY CLAUDE A. FRAZIER

Parent's Guide to Allergy in Children. 1973. Doubleday & Co., New York, New York.

Psychosomatic Aspects of Allergy. 1977. Van Nostrand-Reinhold Company, New York, New York.

Insects and Allergy and What to do About Them. 1980. University of Oklahoma Press, Norman, Oklahoma.

Coping and Living with Food Allergy. 1980. Prentice-Hall Press, Englewood Cliffs, New Jersey.

Coping with Food Allergy. 1974, revised 1985. Times Books, New York, New York.

The Allergy-Free Vegetarian Cookbook

by
Claude A. Frazier, M.D.
and
Dara Llewellyn, Ph.D.

JAIN PUBLISHING COMPANY
Fremont, California

Note: The author and/or publisher shall in no way be held liable for any disorder arising as a direct or indirect result of the ingestion of the recipes in this book. They contain commonly used ingredients, and are to be utilized with the care and discretion of the reader. This book is not intended in any way to be a substitute for medical care; it contains alternate food suggestions for those who must restrict their intake. Any question as to the safety of a particular ingredient should be referred to your physician.

Library of Congress Cataloging-in-Publication Data

Frazier, Claude Albee, 1920-
    The allergy-free vegetarian cookbook / by Claude A. Frazier and Dara Llewellyn.
        p.   cm.
    Includes bibliographical references.
    ISBN 0-87573-033-7
    1. Food allergy—Diet therapy—Recipes. I. Llewellyn, Dara, 1947- . II. Title.
RC588.D53F73   1994
616.97'50654—dc20   94-12369
                                                                              CIP

Acknowledgements

The authors wish to gratefully acknowledge the research and writing of Frieda K. Brown for her earlier work which led to this project.

The authors also wish to acknowledge the following companies and organizations who contributed recipes to this cookbook. If you contact one of these resources directly, please include a self-addressed, stamped envelope.

Allergy Information Association. *The Allergy Cookbook: Diets Unlimited for Limited Diets.* Methuen: New York, 1983.

Arrowhead Mills, Inc. P.O. Box 2059. Hereford, Texas 79045.

CPC International. *Recipes for People with Gluten Intolerance.* Coventry, CT: Best Foods, A Division of CPC International, Inc., 1992.

Dobler, Merri Lou, M.S., R.D. *Gluten Intolerance.* Chicago: The American Dietetic Association, 1991.

Eden Foods, Inc. "Healthy Recipes." Eden Foods, Inc. 701 Tecumseh Road. Clinton, Michigan 49236.

Ener-G Foods, Inc. "Recipes." Seattle: Ener-G Foods, Inc., 1993.

Florida Department of Citrus. Lakeland, Florida 33802-0148.

Frazier, Claude A., M.D. *Coping with Food Allergy.* New York: Times Books, 1974, revised 1985.

Imagine Foods. "Rice Dreams Natural Recipes." Imagine Foods, 350 Cambridge Avenue, Suite 350, Palo Alto, CA 94306.

National Sunflower Agency. 4023 State Street, Bismarck, N.D. 58501.

Nutricia, Inc. "Milk-Free Recipes Using Soyalac and I-Soylac." Nutricia, Inc., 11503 Pierce Street, Riverside, CA 92505.

Ross General Information Series. "Food Sensitivity." Abbott Ross Laboratories, P.O. Box 500010. El Paso, Texas 88550-0010.

U.S.A. Rice Council. "Cooking with Rice." U.S.A. Rice Council. P.O. Box 740123, Houston, TX 77274.

———— . "Light, Lean, Low Fat." U.S.A. Rice Council. P.O. Box 740123, Houston, TX 77274.

———— . "Tasty Rice Recipes for Those with Allergies." U.S.A. Rice Council. P.O. Box 740123, Houston, TX 77274.

Vegetarian Resource Group. P.O. Box 1463. Baltimore, MD 29203.

Washington/Idaho Dry Pea and Lentil Commissions. 5071 Highway 8, West., Moscow, Idaho 83843.

Williams, Margaret L. *Cooking Without: Recipes for the Allergic Child (and Family)*. Ambler, PA: The Gimbal Corporation, 1981.

Note: Recipes were occasionally modified by the authors to fit the allergy-free and vegetarian diet.

Contents

Introduction

Why is it one person can sit down and enjoy a traditional American breakfast of scrambled eggs, toast, and orange juice while another person who sits down to that same breakfast may suffer intense discomfort, pain, and for a certain few, even death?

For a variety of reasons, our bodies can become intolerant of certain foods in our diet. This intolerance often occurs because we tend to overeat certain foods. Symptoms may be so mild or occasional as to be unnoticeable. At other times, symptoms may be so severe as to cause extreme discomfort or severe illness.

Vegetarians avoid certain allergies by virtue of their avoidance of specific food groups. Different categories of vegetarianism are recognized today, depending on which foods are avoided. Although all vegetarians avoid red meat, people who consider themselves partial vegetarians may eat fish as do the ichthyo vegetarians or milk and eggs as do the lacto-ovo vegetarians. It is the vegan who avoids all meat, fish, eggs, or milk products. Today, vegetarianism has become a mainstream life-style choice. The U.S.D.A. has itself acknowledged the importance of vegetables in the diet over meat by publishing a new graphic depicting the recommended proportions to be eaten from each food category and it is drastically different from the old circle that pushed protein as the major component of the American diet.

The Allergy-Free Vegetarian Cookbook

Food Guide Pyramid
A Guide to Daily Food Choices

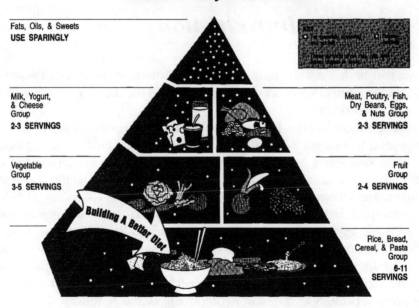

Fats, Oils, & Sweets
USE SPARINGLY

Milk, Yogurt,
& Cheese
Group
2-3 SERVINGS

Meat, Poultry, Fish,
Dry Beans, Eggs,
& Nuts Group
2-3 SERVINGS

Vegetable
Group
3-5 SERVINGS

Fruit
Group
2-4 SERVINGS

Building A Better Diet

Rice, Bread,
Cereal, & Pasta
Group
**6-11
SERVINGS**

Courtesy of U.S.A. Rice Council

But even vegetarians experience problems with some foods. In other words, many of us are allergic to certain foods we eat. In simple terms, an allergy (to food or anything else) is an abnormal reaction to a substance ordinarily tolerated by most persons, a case of overreaction by the body's protective mechanism.

Allergeric symptoms which are severe enough will send us to a physician for medical diagnosis and treatment. But for many of us, we simply become aware that certain foods don't treat us well once they are in our systems. For some, the culprit may be milk; for another it may be strawberries. Most often wheat, milk, eggs, and corn are the offenders. The obvious solution, of course, is simply to omit that food from our diet. And that can be hard if that food is one of our favorites.

One encouraging note is that because intolerance or sensitivity to certain foods often comes about because of prolonged or over-exposure to that food, a period of abstinence (avoiding the food culprit) followed by limited and moderate consumption may allow us to go back to eating that particular food. In certain cases, however, the intolerance may be so severe that complete avoidance is our only healthy solution.

There are a number of other factors which can affect allergy disease, including food allergies: amount and duration of exposure (as just mentioned), heredity, potency of the allergens, a person's physical condition, emotional stress, seasonal factors, and, of specific significance here, cross reactions (between foods).

Cross reactions occur because foods, like people, come in families, and these family relationships have important repercussions for the allergic. For example, an individual who is allergic to orange juice, may also be sensitive to lemons and grapefruits. An individual who wants to follow a lacto-ovo vegetarian diet but who happens to be allergic to chicken may not only have to avoid eating chicken, but may also find eating eggs can cause problems, such as eczema, because chicken and eggs are in the same family of foods. Even honey, a favorite sweetener, may produce a cross reaction if the bees have fed upon buckwheat blossoms, and the honey is then eaten by a buckwheat-sensitive individual. Paying attention to all these factors in relationship to our allergic responses can help us to become knowledgeable about our sensitivity.

Any food may be the cause of allergic reactions but the following foods are more potent allergens than other foods:

milk	fish and shellfish
eggs	berries
wheat	peas and legumes
chocolate	citrus fruits
nuts	corn

The fact that a food is extremely nutritious does not keep it from being a potent allergen, as the above list demonstrates. Vegetarians may be happy to discover that vegetables are, perhaps, less often seen as potent sources of allergens. But among non-grain vegetables—legumes (including the peanut), tomatoes, celery, cabbage, cauliflower, white potatoes, mushrooms, carrots, squash, and lettuce are generally considered the chief villains for producing sensitivity.

The simplest way to determine which foods you are sensitive to is to keep a food diary, keeping account of what you eat, when you eat, and what symptoms you feel. Allergic reactions can be delayed or immediate, so keeping a food diary over a period of time (two to three weeks) will allow you to see the correlation between what you eat and how you feel. It establishes a record which allows you to examine the relationship between food and symptom.

Once the suspect foods are identified, you can modify your diet to eliminate those foods entirely. Once the symptoms disappear, the foods can be introduced on a moderate and limited basis, with care being taken to continue the food diary, noting the recurrence of any symptoms. This approach is one that you can undertake at home if your food allergy symptoms are not too severe.

The cause-and-effect relationship between foods and allergies, unfortunately, is not all that clear. Reactions may occur hours later or even two or three days later. Consulting an allergy specialist may be the onlyway to get a grip on symptoms that have become chronic, even violent.

The allergy specialist will begin by taking note of your medical history and giving you a complete physical examination with special attention to the bodily system(s) affected. The doctor will be looking for allergy-related clues such as the appearance of your mucous membranes, dark and puffy circles under the eyes called allergic shiners, or mouth breathing and snoring. Laboratory tests called for may include blood, nasal, or stool smears. Among the allergic, eosinophils are usually found in these tests. These are red, staining cells ("eosin" means red and "phil" means love—the cell loves the red stain).

These skin tests are reliable with inhalant allergies and so are useful to ensure that such allergens are not working in conjunction with food allergens. The scratch (or prick) test consists of making a tiny scratch on the skin, usually on the patient's back or his inner arm below the elbow. A drop of extract of the substance to be tested is then applied. The patient waits for about twenty minutes until the results can be read. If nothing happens at the scratch site, the test is considered negative. If the skin at the scratch site becomes irritated (reddened or raised), then the patient is considered potentially allergic to the substance. Intradermal skin tests are more accurate than scratch tests. These tests are performed by injecting an extract under the skin. Tests are read in ten to fifteen minutes.

Because skin tests are not generally reliable in food sensitivity (with the exception of skin tests for eggs), a food diary and elimination diet will also be part of the diagnostic process. The re-introduction of foods is a trial and error procedure, working back to a more normal diet with as few proscribed items as possible. On this return trip, those foods that cause illness are discovered. Symptoms may be immediate to one food or occur several hours later to another food. One should watch for a flare up of allergy symptoms while trying a new food. Food allergy can affect a person in many ways: wheezing, an increase in nasal congestion or postnasal drainage, headaches, vomiting, diarrhea, or skin rash.

Certain foods are associated with particular symptoms. For example, I have found that chocolate and cola drinks often tend to cause headaches (discussed further in my book *Coping with Food Allergy*). Also, a person may be allergic to raw food (apples, potatoes) but can eat that food when cooked. The elimination diet is both test and remedy, a technique of discovery and relief.

Armed with the knowledge of what we need to eliminate from our diet, we can turn to the pleasurable chore of figuring out how to cook delicious meals minus certain foods that we have been used to eating. Hundreds of allergy-free recipes exist today as a result of allergic individuals learning to cook while avoiding the foods they cannot tolerate. We have tried to include a wide variety of tasty vegetarian dishes to satisfy every phase of a meal: breads or pastries, main dishes, side dishes, soups and sauces, and desserts. Enjoy!

CHAPTER ONE

Wheat-Free and Gluten-Free Cooking

Wheat intolerance affects many individuals in the United States where it is eaten in large amounts. Wheat, like milk and eggs, contains several allergenic components, the main two being gluten and starch. Gluten is probably the more potent allergen and causes the most damage. There are people who simply cannot handle gluten, either because of a specific allergy or because of a malabsorption problem of the gastrointestinal system. Once a wheat or gluten intolerance is diagnosed, the only effective treatment is avoidance. Consult your physician first so other problems or intolerances may be ruled out.

Tracking down the presence of wheat and gluten sources in your diet, however, can be tricky. The first step is to know that gluten occurs not only in wheat but also, in lesser amounts, in rye, oats, and barley. Vegetarians who rely on grains as a larger percentage of their diet must be alert to the presence of gluten in all these grains. If intolerant of gluten, you must avoid all foods, such as bread and pasta, that are made with these grain products. Even when eating out, you must be alert to foods in which one of these four grains is a component.

The next step in avoiding gluten requires reading the list of ingredients on all the prepared foods you buy, an annoying but necessary precaution. The presence of gluten may be disguised under a number of aliases. Watch out for items listed as hydrolyzed vegetable protein (HVP), wheat starch, modified food starch, monosodium glutamate, malt flavorings, distilled vinegar, emulsifiers, and stabilizers, all of which may contain gluten or one of its components, gliadin.

After you have learned to recognize the presence of these grain products and know to avoid them, then you can learn how to substitute other products to take their place. A number of food companies such as Ener-G Foods market products with wheat and gluten intolerance in mind. Otherwise, grains and vegetables such as rice and potatoes may also serve to replace those grains which contain gluten.

This chapter addresses these concerns. It begins with a list of substitutions you can make from your own pantry, followed by a listing of all the important terms you may need to know. The tasty recipes are included from which you may create complete meals entirely free of gluten products. Finally, recipes involving special products available in the market today are included.

Happy and healthy eating!

Gluten Substitutions

Baking Substitutions for 1 cup of wheat flour

- $7/8$ cup rice (white or brown) flour
- $5/8$ cup potato starch flour
- 1 cup soy flour & $1/4$ cup potato starch flour

- $1/2$ cup soy flour & $1/2$ cup potato starch flour
- 1 cup corn flour
- $3/4$-1 scant cup fine cornmeal

Thickening Agents Substitutions for 1 tablespoon wheat flour:

- $1^1/2$ teaspoon cornstarch
- $1^1/2$ teaspoon potato starch
- $1^1/2$ teaspoon arrowroot starch

- 1 tablespoon white or brown rice flour
- 2 teaspoons quick-cooking tapioca
- $1^1/2$ teaspoons sweet rice flour

The above substitutions were drawn from *Coping with Food Allergy* by Claude A. Frazier, M.D. (published by Times Books) and from a revised edition of *Gluten Intolerance* by Merri Lou Dobler, M.S., R.D. (published by the American Dietetic Association).

List of Important Terms

- **Gluten:** a plant protein mixture found in grains like wheat, rye, oats, and barley.

- **Gliadin:** a component of gluten which is toxic to certain individuals.

- **Glutenin:** another component of gluten which is more digestible than gliadin.

- **HVP (hydrolyzed vegetable protein):** contains gluten.

- **Malt:** a grain form, usually barley, contains gluten.

- **Gums:** xantham or guar gum may substitute for gluten in yeast breads.

Wheat-Free and Gluten-Free Cooking

⟨⟨ Breads, Pastries, and

Other Such Recipes ⟩⟩

GLUTEN-FREE PIZZA

1	cup rice flour
1/2	cup Argo or Kingsford corn starch
1	teaspoon baking powder
1/4	teaspoon salt
3/4	cup milk
1/4	cup Mazola corn oil
1/3	cup prepared gluten-free pizza sauce
1	cup (4 oz.) shredded mozzarella cheese

Each serving provides:
300 calories
7 g protein
37 g carbohydrate
15 g total fat
6 g polyunsaturated fat
4 g saturated fat
20 mg cholesterol
390 mg sodium

1. Preheat oven to 425° F.
2. In medium bowl combine rice flour, corn starch, baking powder, and salt. Stir in milk and corn oil to form a very soft dough. Spread on cookie sheet to form a 10-inch circle, 1/4-inch thick. Bake 12 to 14 minutes or until lightly browned around edge. Remove from oven.
3. Spread sauce over crust; sprinkle with cheese. (Bake 5 to 7 minutes or until cheese is bubbly.) Makes 6 servings.

(CPC International)

CORN STARCH CREPES

2   eggs
3/4   cup milk
1   tablespoon corn oil
1/4   teaspoon salt
1/2   cup corn starch
      No Stick cooking spray

> **Each unfilled**
> **crepe provides:**
> 50 calories
> 2 g protein
> 6 g carbohydrate
> 3 g total fat
> 1 g polyunsaturated fat
> 1 g saturated fat
> 40 mg cholesterol
> 65 mg sodium

1. In blender, combine eggs, milk, corn oil, salt, and corn starch; blend 30 seconds or until smooth.
2. Spray 6-inch skillet or crepe pan with cooking spray. Heat well over medium-high heat. Pour about 2 tablespoons batter into center of skillet, rotating quickly to evenly coat bottom. Cook about 30 seconds or until edge begins to brown and pull away from pan. Carefully turn crepe; cook 30 seconds longer.
3. Slide out of skillet onto wax paper-lined tray. Repeat with remaining batter. Use crepes for recipes provided or fill as desired. Makes twelve 6-inch crepes.

Note: To store, layer crepes between sheets of wax paper; cover tightly with plastic wrap. Refrigerate up to 5 days or freeze up to 1 month. For easier rolling, microwave a few crepes at a time on High (100%) 30 seconds or until slightly warm and pliable.

(CPC International)

SOUTHERN CORN BREAD

	No Stick cooking spray
2	cups yellow corn meal
2	tablespoons sugar
1½	teaspoons baking powder
1	teaspoon salt
2	eggs, beaten
⅔	cup milk
¼	cup corn oil
1	can (8 oz.) creamed corn

Each serving (without chilies) provides:	Each serving (with chilies) provides:
220 calories	230 calories
5 g protein	5 g protein
33 g carbohydrate	33 g carbohydrate
8 g total fat	8 g total fat
4 g unsaturated fat	4 g unsaturated fat
2 g saturated fat	2 g saturated fat
50 mg cholesterol	50 mg cholesterol
390 mg sodium	540 mg sodium

1. Spray 8-inch square baking pan with cooking spray.
2. In medium bowl combine corn meal, sugar, baking powder and salt.
3. In small bowl combine eggs, milk, corn oil, and creamed corn; stir into corn meal mixture just until moistened.
4. Turn into baking pan. Bake in 400° F. oven 20 to 25 minutes or until lightly browned. Makes 9 servings.

CHILI CORN BREAD: Follow recipe for Corn Bread. Stir in 1 can (4 oz.) chopped green chilies into batter.

(CPC International)

CHEESE PUFFS

No Stick cooking spray
1 cup water
¼ cup (½ stick) margarine
¼ teaspoon ground red pepper
¼ teaspoon salt
1 cup corn starch
3 eggs
1½ cups (6 oz.) shredded Cheddar cheese

Each cheese puff provides:
35 calories
1 g protein
3 g carbohydrate
2 g total fat
0 g polyunsaturated fat
1 g saturated fat
20 mg cholesterol
45 mg sodium

1. Spray cookie sheets with cooking spray; set aside.
2. In 2-quart saucepan combine water, margarine, red pepper, and salt; bring to a boil over medium heat.
3. Remove from heat. Add corn starch all at once, stirring constantly until mixture forms a ball.
4. Add eggs, one at a time, beating well after each addition. Stir in cheese.
5. Drop mixture by rounded teaspoonfuls 2 inches apart on prepared baking sheets.
6. Bake in 400° F. oven 20 minutes or until puffed and golden. Serve warm. Makes 48.

Make-Ahead Tip: Cheese Puffs can be made ahead and frozen in tightly sealed food storage container. To serve, place on baking sheet and heat in 300° F oven 10 minutes or until heated through.

(CPC International)

PIZZA RICE CAKES

4	rice cakes
⅓	cup pizza sauce
¼	cup each sliced ripe olives, diced green pepper, & sliced mushrooms
⅓	cup shredded mozzarella cheese

> **Each serving provides:**
> 86 calories
> 4.1 g protein
> 9.5 g carbohydrate
> 3.2 g fat
> 5 mg cholesterol
> 249 mg sodium

1. Place rice cakes on baking sheet. Spread pizza sauce evenly on each rice cake; top with remaining ingredients.
2. Bake at 400° F. for 10 minutes. Serve immediately.
   Makes 4 servings.

(U.S.A. Rice Council)

SIMPLE ONE-LOAF BARLEY BREAD

1   cup warm water
1   package dry yeast
2   tablespoons honey
1   teaspoon sea salt (optional)
1   cup Arrowhead Mills Barley flour
2   teaspoons Arrowhead Mills Canola Oil
2   cups Arrowhead Mills Oat Flour

1.   Mix first five ingredients together and let stand 10 minutes. Stir down and let stand 15 minutes.
2.   Add oil and flour. Knead for 3 minutes. Shape into loaf. Let rise in pan until double in size.
3.   Bake at 350° F. for 45 minutes or until toothpick inserted in the center comes out clean.

Note: This bread is somewhat flat but very tasty.

(Arrowhead Mills, Inc.)

MILLET BREAD

1   cup plain yogurt or buttermilk
¹/₄   cup butter
1   tablespoon honey
1   package dry yeast
¹/₄   cup warm water
2   eggs
2   cups Arrowhead Mills Millet Flour
¹/₂   cup Arrowhead Mills Soy Flour

1. Combine yogurt and butter in saucepan, heating slowly to melt butter. Dissolve yeast and honey in the warm water; add yogurt mixture and blend.
2. Beat in eggs; add flours and beat well.
3. Pour into well-oiled 4-inch × 8-inch loaf pan and let rise for 45 minutes.
4. Bake at 375° F. for 40-45 minutes or until done. Cool before cutting.

(Arrowhead Mills, Inc.)

Wheat-Free and Gluten-Free Cooking

Main Dishes

CREPE LASAGNA

Corn Starch Crepes batter (see Corn
Starch Crepe recipe, p. 11)
1   container (15 oz.) low-fat ricotta cheese
2   cups (8 oz.) shredded, part-skim mozzarella
       cheese, divided
¹/₄   cup grated Parmesan cheese
1   egg
1   jar (14 oz.) prepared gluten-free spaghetti sauce

Each serving provides:
400 calories
24 g protein
27 g carbohydrate
22 g total fat
3 g polyunsaturated fat
10 g saturated fat
160 mg cholesterol
810 mg sodium

1. For crepes, spray 9" skillet with cooking spray; heat well over medium-high heat. Pour ¹/₂ cup crepe batter into center of skillet, rotating quickly to evenly coat bottom.
2. Cook about 1 minute or until edge begins to brown and pull away from pan. Carefully turn crepe; cook 1 minute longer. Slide out of skillet onto wax paper-lined tray. Repeat to make 3 9-inch crepes.
3. In medium bowl, combine ricotta cheese, 1¹/₂ cups mozzarella, Parmesan, and egg; mix well.
4. Spoon ¹/₄ of the spaghetti sauce in bottom of 9" round cake pan or baking dish. Top with 1 crepe, half the cheese mixture and additional sauce. Repeat layer once, ending with crepe. Top with remaining sauce and mozzarella. Bake in 350° F. oven 35 minutes or until hot and bubbly. Let stand 10 minutes before serving. Cut into wedges. Makes 6 servings.

(CPC International)

LENTIL LOAF

2	cups lentils, cooked
2	cups tomato sauce
$1/2$	cup onions, chopped
$1/2$	cup celery, chopped
$3/4$	cup Ener-G Gluten-free Rice Flakes
$1/2$	teaspoon garlic powder
$1/4$	teaspoon Italian seasonings
$1/4$	teaspoon celery seed
	pepper and salt to taste
$1/2$	cup walnuts, chopped (optional)

1. Mix all the ingredients together in a large bowl.
2. Press lightly into oiled loaf pan.
3. Bake 45 minutes in 350° F. oven.
4. Slice and serve.

(Vegetarian Resource Group)

SPLIT PEA AND VEGETABLE CURRY BOMBAY

Each serving provides:
228 calories

1	cup onion, chopped
2	cloves of garlic, minced
1	tablespoon curry powder
1	teaspoon ground cumin
1/4	cup salad oil
1	cup yellow split peas, rinsed and drained
3	cups water
3	tablespoons lemon juice

1	teaspoon salt
1/2	teaspoon white pepper
1	small eggplant (about 1 lb.), cut into 1/2 inch cubes
1	small cauliflower (about 1 1/2 lb.), cut into florets
1/2	cup each raisins and coconut
1/4	cup parsley, chopped

1. In a large heavy pan, cook onion, garlic, curry, and cumin in oil until onion is tender.
2. Add split peas, water, lemon juice, salt, and pepper.
3. Cover and bring to a boil; reduce heat; simmer 15 minutes.
4. Add eggplant, cauliflower, and raisins, then simmer 30 minutes more until vegetables and peas are tender.
5. Stir in coconut and parsley.
   Makes about 8 cups, 8 servings.

(Washington and Idaho Dry Pea and Lentil Commissions)

MACARONI & CHEESE

Each serving provides:
290 calories
13 g protein
37 g carbohydrate
10 g total fat
1 g polyunsaturated fat
6 g saturated fat
35 mg cholesterol
400 mg sodium

    Mazola No Stick cooking spray
2   tablespoons Argo or Kingsford corn starch
$^1/_2$ teaspoon salt
$^1/_2$ teaspoon dry mustard
$^1/_4$ teaspoon pepper
$2^1/_4$ cups skim milk
$1^1/_2$ cups (6 oz.) shredded Cheddar cheese
8   oz. gluten-free pasta (elbows or shells),
    slightly undercooked and drained
    Corn flake crumbs (optional)

1. Spray 2-quart casserole with cooking spray.
2. In medium saucepan combine corn starch, salt, mustard, and pepper. Stir in milk until smooth. Stirring constantly, bring to a boil over medium heat and boil 1 minute.
3. Remove from heat. Stir in cheese until melted.
4. Add macaroni. Turn into casserole. If desired, sprinkle with corn flake crumbs.
5. Bake uncovered in 375° F. oven 25 minutes or until lightly browned. Makes 6 servings. (CPC International)

RICE PRIMAVERA

2	teaspoons olive oil
1	clove garlic
2	cups broccoli florets
1	cup each sliced zucchini and sliced fresh mushrooms
1	medium tomato, seeded and chopped
1/4	cup snipped fresh parsley
1/3	cup light reduced calorie mayonnaise
1/2	cup skim milk
1/4	cup freshly grated Parmesan cheese
1/4	teaspoon ground white or red pepper
3	cups cooked rice

Each serving provides:
255 calories
7.5 g protein
35.4 g carbohydrate
9.5 g fat
35.4 g dietary fiber
11 mg cholesterol
607 mg sodium

1. Heat garlic with oil in large skillet over medium-high heat; discard garlic.
2. Cook broccoli, zucchini, and mushrooms in oil until almost tender crisp.
3. Add tomatoes and parsley; cook one minute longer. Remove vegetables and set aside.
4. Place mayonnaise in same skillet; stir in milk, cheese, and pepper. Cook over medium heat, stirring until smooth.
5. Add rice and toss to coat. Stir in reserved vegetables; heat through. Serve immediately.

(U.S.A. Rice Council)

BRUNCH RICE

1	teaspoon margarine
3/4	cup each shredded carrots, diced green pepper, and sliced fresh mushrooms
6	egg whites, beaten
2	eggs, beaten
1/2	cup skim milk
1/2	teaspoon salt
1/4	teaspoon ground black pepper
3	cups cooked brown rice
1/2	cup (2 oz.) shredded cheddar cheese

Each serving provides:
212 calories
11.4 g protein
27 g carbohydrate
6.5 g fat
2.5 g dietary fiber
79 mg cholesterol
35.3 mg sodium

1. Melt margarine in large skillet over medium-high heat until hot. Add carrots, green pepper, and mushrooms; cook 2 minutes.
2. Combine egg whites, eggs, milk, salt, and black pepper in small bowl.
3. Reduce heat to medium and pour egg mixture over vegetables; continue stirring 1 1/2 to 2 minutes.
4. Add rice and cheese; stir to gently separate grains. Heat 2 minutes. Serve immediately.

Microwave Oven Instructions:

1. Combine carrots, green pepper, mushrooms, and margarine in 2½ quart microproof baking dish.
2. Cover and cook on HIGH 4 minutes.
3. Combine egg whites, eggs, milk, salt, and black pepper in small mixing bowl; pour over vegetables. Cook on HIGH 4 minutes, stirring with fork after each minute to cut cooked eggs into small pieces.
4. Stir in rice; cook on HIGH about 1 minute until heated.

(U.S.A. Rice Council)

Wheat-Free and Gluten-Free Cooking

ꙮ Side Dishes ꙮ

MAWASH LENTILS

1½   cups cooked lentils
1½   cups cooked long-grain white rice
4   tablespoons butter or margarine
2   large onions, thinly sliced
½   teaspoon pepper
½   teaspoon salt

1. Cook rice and lentils.
2. Saute onion in the hot butter to a delicate brown.
3. Combine thoroughly drained rice and lentils.
4. Add salt and pepper and mix. Top with browned onion.
    Yields: 5 servings

(Washington and Idaho Pea and Lentil Commissions)

BLACK BEANS AND RICE SALAD

2	cups cooked rice, cooled to room temperature
1	cup each cooked black beans and chopped fresh tomato
¹/₂	cup (2 oz.) shredded cheddar cheese
1	tablespoon snipped fresh parsley
¹/₄	cup prepared light Italian dressing
1	tablespoon fresh lime juice
	Lettuce leaves

Each serving provides:
209 calories
7.4 g protein
0.7 g fat
43.1 g carbohydrate
3.2 g dietary fiber
560 mg sodium
0 mg cholesterol

1. Combine rice, beans, tomato, cheese, and parsley in large bowl.
2. Pour dressing and lime juice over rice mixture; toss.
3. Serve on lettuce leaves.

(U.S.A. Rice Council)

ZUCCHINI FRITTERS

1   large zucchini or several small
¼   cup diced onion
½   cup soy or rice flour
¼   teaspoon salt
¼   teaspoon baking soda
1   egg
¼   cup milk (may substitute soy milk)
2   tablespoons olive oil

1. Wash and grate zucchini with skin on. Paper towel out moisture.
2. Mix in flour, salt, and baking powder. Add one egg beaten, milk, and onion.
3. Stir until batter is consistency of pancake batter.
4. Heat olive oil in skillet and drop approximately ⅛ cup of drop batter in skillet. Fry until golden brown.

Wheat-Free and Gluten-Free Cooking

❧ Soups, Sauces, and Gravies ❧

CREAM OF BROCCOLI SOUP

<table>
<tr><td>

4   tablespoons Mazola margarine
1   medium onion, chopped
1   clove garlic, chopped
2   tablespoons Argo or Kingsford corn starch
1   package (10 oz.) frozen chopped broccoli, partially thawed
1   can (14 oz.) chicken broth
1   cup milk
</td></tr>
</table>

1/4   teaspoon salt
1/8   teaspoon pepper

Each serving provides:
140 calories
5 g protein
8 g carbohydrate
10 g total fat
3 g polyunsaturated fat
2 g saturated fat
5 mg cholesterol
560 mg sodium

1. In 3-quart saucepan melt margarine over medium heat. Add onion and garlic; saute 5 minutes or until tender. Stir in corn starch until smooth.
2. Add broccoli, chicken broth, milk, salt and pepper. Stirring occasionally, bring to a boil over medium high heat and boil 1 minute.
3. Carefully blend hot mixture about 1/3 at a time until smooth.
4. Return to saucepan and heat through. Makes 6 servings.

Variations: Substitute a 10 oz. pkg. of frozen asparagus, spinach, peas, corn, carrots, cauliflower, or squash for the broccoli.

(CPC International)

CHILI CON LENTILS

Each serving provides:
268 calories

5   cups water
1   can (16 oz.) chickpeas, drained
1   cup chopped onion
1/2 cup chopped celery
1   large clove garlic, minced
2   teaspoon ground cumin
1   teaspoon salt
1   pound (2 1/3 cups) lentils,
    rinsed and drained

1   can (16 oz.) kidney beans, drained
1   can (16 oz.) tomatoes, cut up
1/2 cup chopped carrots
1/2 cup chopped green pepper
1   tablespoon chili powder
1   teaspoon crushed red pepper flakes

1. Combine all ingredients in a large heavy pan.
2. Cover; bring to a boil and reduce heat and simmer 30 minutes or so until lentils are tender.
3. Top with shredded cheddar cheese.
   Makes about 11 cups.

(Washington and Idaho Dry Pea Lentil Commissions)

LEMON SAUCE

¹/₂   cup sugar
1   tablespoon cornstarch or
    2 Tbsp rice flour
¹/₈   teaspoon salt
1   cup boiling water
2   tablespoons butter or
    milk-free margarine
1¹/₂ tablespoon lemon juice

1. Blend dry ingredients in sauce pan.
2. Gradually add boiling water, stirring constantly. Cook over low heat 5 minutes until thick and clear.
3. Remove from heat. Add butter and lemon juice.
   Yields: 6 servings, ¹/₄ cup each.

Each serving provides:
100 calories
0 g protein
17 g carbohydrate
4 g fat
0 mg cholesterol
97 mg sodium

(The American Dietetic Association's *Gluten Intolerance*)

GAZPACHO SOUP

Prep. Time: 10 minutes
Chill: 1 hour
Yield: 5 servings

1	28 oz, can Eden Organic Crushed Tomatoes
1	cup water
2	tablespoons onion, minced
1/2	cup green pepper, diced
1/2	cup red pepper, diced
4	cups cucumbers, peeled, seeded, and cut into chunks
1/2	cup green onions, diced
3	cloves garlic, pressed
3	tablespoons Eden Red Wine Vinegar
2	tablespoons Eden Shoyu Soy Sauce
1	teaspoon cumin
3	tablespoons lemon juice
3	tablespoons lime juice
1	teaspoon basil, minced
1	teaspoon dill, minced

1. Combine all ingredients and chill for at least 1 hour before serving.

(Eden Foods)

SALSA

Prep. Time: 10 minutes
Cooking Time: 45 minutes
Yield: 4 cups

1	tablespoon Eden Olive Oil
1	cup onion, diced
2	garlic cloves, pressed
½	cup green pepper, diced
½	cup red pepper, diced
1	28 oz. can Eden Organic Crushed Tomatoes
2	teaspoons Eden Red Wine Vinegar
1	tablespoon yellow hot pepper, diced
1	teaspoon cumin
¼	teaspoon black pepper
1	tablespoon cilantro, chopped
¼	teaspoon cayenne pepper

1. Heat oil; saute onion, garlic, green and red pepper until onions are translucent.
2. Add tomatoes and red wine vinegar.
3. Simmer for 30 minutes.
4. Add hot pepper, cumin, black pepper and cilantro.
5. Simmer for 5-10 minutes more.
6. Remove from heat and add cayenne.
7. Chill to blend flavors.

(Eden Foods)

HOMEMADE BARBEQUE SAUCE

Prep. Time: 5 minutes	
Cooking Time: 5 minutes	
Yield: $^2/_3$ cup	

1   tablespoon Eden Hot Mustard
3   tablespoons honey
2   teaspoons tamari
1   teaspoon black pepper
$^1/_2$ cup Eden Organic Spaghetti Sauce
1   tablespoon Eden Apple Cider Vinegar
2   teaspoons water

1.   Mix all ingredients well.
2.   Simmer 5 minutes.

(Eden Foods)

Wheat-Free and Gluten-Free Cooking

ᑐᑕ Desserts ᑐᑕ

CARROT CAKE

Mazola No Stick cooking spray
1   cup white rice flour
¹/₄ cup Argo or Kingsford corn starch
1   teaspoon baking soda
1   teaspoon cinnamon
¹/₄ teaspoon ground ginger
¹/₄ teaspoon salt
2   eggs
1   cup sugar
¹/₂ cup Hellmann's or Best Food mayonnaise
1   can (8 oz.) crushed pineapple in juice, undrained
1¹/₂ cups shredded carrots
¹/₂ cup chopped walnuts
Cream Cheese Frosting (recipe follows)

1. Spray 9-inch square baking pan with cooking spray.
2. In medium bowl combine rice flour, corn starch, baking soda, cinnamon, ginger, and salt.
3. In large bowl with mixer at medium speed, beat eggs, sugar, mayonnaise, and pineapple with juice.

Each serving provides:
300 calories
4 g protein
39 g carbohydrate
15 g total fat
6 g polyunsaturated fat
4 g saturated fat
50 mg cholesterol
210 mg sodium

Gradually beat in flour mixture until blended. Stir in carrots and nuts. Pour into prepared pan.

4. Bake in 350° F. oven 40 minutes or until toothpick inserted in center comes out clean. Cool on wire rack. Frost with Cream Cheese Frosting. Makes 12 servings.

CREAM CHEESE FROSTING: In small bowl beat 4 oz. softened cream cheese, $\frac{1}{3}$ cup confectioner's sugar and 1 teaspoon orange juice until smooth. Spread over top of cooled cake.

(CPC International)

CHEESE BLINTZES WITH BLUEBERRY SAUCE

Corn Starch crepes
(See earlier recipe on p. 11)
2 packages (7½ oz.) farmer cheese
1 egg

3 tablespoons sugar
4 tablespoons Mazola margarine
   Blueberry Sauce (recipe
   follows)

Each serving (with ⅓ cup sauce) provides:
350 calories
17 g protein
41 g carbohydrate
14 g total fat
4 g polyunsaturated fat
3 g saturated fat
115 mg cholesterol
230 mg sodium

1. Prepare Corn Starch crepes; set aside.
2. In medium bowl combine farmer cheese, egg, and sugar.
3. Place two rounded tablespoons filling in center of each crepe. Fold top and bottom edges into center, then fold sides over to form an egg roll-like packet. Repeat with each crepe.
4. In large skillet melt 2 tablespoons margarine over medium heat. Place half the blintzes seam-side down in skillet. Cook turning once, 8 to 10 minutes or until lightly browned on both sides. Repeat with remaining margarine and blintzes.
5. Serve warm with Blueberry Sauce. Makes 6 servings.

BLUEBERRY SAUCE: In 2-quart saucepan combine ¼ cup sugar and 1 tablespoon Argo or Kingsford corn starch. Stir in ½ cup orange juice or water, then 2 cups fresh or frozen blueberries. Stirring constantly, bring to a boil over medium-high heat and boil one minute. Stir in an additional 1 cup blueberries; cook 1 minute longer. Spoon over blintzes. Makes 2 cups.

(CPC International)

EASY PINEAPPLE CHEESECAKE

Mazola No Stick Cooking Spray
2   packages (8 oz. each) reduced-calorie cream cheese, softened
1   cup sugar
1/2 cup milk
3   eggs
1/4 cup Argo or Kingsford corn starch
2   teaspoons vanilla extract
1   can (8 oz.) crushed pineapple in juice, drained, juice reserved
    Cinnamon

Each serving provides:
220 calories
6 g protein
24 g carbohydrate
11 g total fat
0 g polyunsaturated fat
6 g saturated fat
90 mg cholesterol
180 mg sodium

1. Spray 9-inch square baking dish with cooking spray.
2. In blender combine cream cheese, sugar, milk, eggs, corn starch, vanilla, and reserved pineapple juice. Blend 1 minute or until smooth, scraping down sides once. Pour into prepared baking dish.
3. Spoon pineapple evenly over top (pineapple sinks into batter). Sprinkle with cinnamon.
4. Bake in 300° F. oven 59 to 60 minutes or until set. Cool on wire rack 1 hour. Refrigerate.
    Makes 12 servings.

(CPC International)

EASY VANILLA PUDDING

	Each ¹/₂ cup serving (vanilla) provides:	Each ¹/₂ cup serving (chocolate) provides:
	200 calories	260 calories
	4 g protein	5 g protein
	26 g carbohydrate	40 g carbohydrate
	9 g total fat	9 g total fat
	2 g polyunsaturated fat	2 g polyunsaturated fat
	4 g saturated fat	4 g saturated fat
	20 mg cholesterol	20 mg cholesterol
	170 mg sodium	190 mg sodium

¹/₃ cup sugar
¹/₄ cup Argo or Kingsford corn starch
¹/₈ teaspoon salt
2 ¹/₄ cups milk
2 tablespoons Mazola margarine
1 teaspoon vanilla

1. In medium saucepan combine sugar, cornstarch, and salt. Gradually stir in milk until smooth. Stirring constantly, bring to a boil over medium heat and boil 1 minute.
2. Remove from heat. Stir in margarine and vanilla.
3. Pour into serving bowls. Cover, refrigerate. Makes about 2 ¹/₂ cups.

EASY CHOCOLATE PUDDING: Increase sugar to ²/₃ cup and add 3 tablespoons unsweetened cocoa with cornstarch. Makes 2 ¹/₂ cups.

(CPC International)

44

PEANUT BUTTER CEREAL TREATS

Each serving provides:
60 calories
1 g protein
9 g carbohydrate
2 g total fat
1 g polyunsaturated fat
0 g saturated fat
0 mg cholesterol
45 mg sodium

4   cups crispy rice or cornflake cereal
$1/2$ cup sugar
$1/2$ cup light or dark Karo corn syrup
$1/2$ cup Skippy Creamy or Super Chunk peanut butter

1.   Line 9-inch square baking pan with plastic wrap.
2.   Pour cereal into large bowl.
3.   In medium saucepan combine sugar and corn syrup. Stirring occasionally, bring to a boil over medium heat and boil 1 minute. Remove from heat.
4.   Add peanut butter, stir until completely melted. Pour over cereal; stir to coat well. Press evenly into prepared pan.
5.   Cool about 15 minutes. Invert onto cutting board; remove plastic wrap. Cut into squares. Makes 36 squares.

Microwave Directions: Prepare pan as directed above. Pour cereal into large bowl. In 2-quart microwavable bowl combine sugar, corn syrup, and peanut butter. Microwave on HIGH (100%), stirring twice, $3^1/2$ to 4 minutes or until mixture is smooth and sugar is dissolved. Continue as directed above.

(CPC International)

CHOCOLATE MOUSSE CAKE

Mazola No Stick Cooking Spray
1   package (8 oz.) semisweet chocolate
1/2   cup (1 stick) Mazola margarine
6   eggs, separated
1/3   cup sugar
2   tablespoons Argo or Kingsford corn starch
Confectioners sugar

Each serving provides:
280 calories
5 g protein
21 g carbohydrate
21 g total fat
4 g polyunsaturated fat
7 g saturated fat
130 mg cholesterol
135 mg sodium

1. Spray 9-inch springform pan with cooking spray; dust lightly with additional corn starch.
2. In small saucepan combine chocolate and margarine. Cook over low heat, stirring frequently, just until chocolate melts. Pour into large bowl; cool to room temperature.
3. In medium bowl with mixer at high speed, beat egg whites until foamy. Gradually add sugar, beating until soft peaks form.
4. Add egg yolks to chocolate mixture; stir until blended. Stir in corn starch. Gently fold in egg whites until thoroughly blended. Pour into prepared pan.
5. Bake in 300° F. oven 40 minutes or until set. Run knife around edge. Cool on wire rack. Remove side of pan. Sprinkle with confectioners sugar. Makes 10 servings.

(CPC International)

APRICOT UPSIDE DOWN CAKE

<table>
<tr><td></td><td>Each serving provides:</td></tr>
</table>

¹/₄	cup salad oil or melted, milk-free margarine
¹/₂	cup firmly packed brown sugar
1	can (1 lb., 4 oz.) apricot halves, water or juice pack, drained (save juice)
¹/₄	cup syrup drained from fruit
3	egg yolks
¹/₂	cup sugar
1	cup rice flour
2	teaspoons baking powder
¹/₄	teaspoon salt
2	tablespoons salad oil or melted, milk-free margarine
1	teaspoon alcohol-free vanilla extract
3	egg whites, stiffly beaten

Each serving provides:
275 calories
4 g protein
11 g total fat
41 g carbohydrate
159 mg sodium
71 mg cholesterol

1. Preheat oven to 325° F. oven (slow).
2. Pour 1/4 cup oil into 8" square pan. Sprinkle with brown sugar. Arrange apricot halves over brown sugar.
3. Beat egg yolks and sugar together until thick and lemon colored.

4. Sift together flour, baking powder, and salt. Add to egg yolk mixture with 2 tablespoons oil, fruit syrup, and vanilla. Mix just until smooth.
5. Fold in stiffly beaten egg whites. Pour batter over fruit in pan.
6. Bake 40 minutes. Cool 10 minutes. Turn upside down on serving plate.
    Makes 9 servings.

Variation: Other fruit may be substituted for apricots.

(The American Dietetic Association *Gluten Intolerance*)

CHIFFON CAKE

<table>
<tr><td>³/₄</td><td>cup rice flour</td></tr>
<tr><td>³/₄</td><td>cup sugar</td></tr>
<tr><td>2</td><td>teaspoons baking powder</td></tr>
<tr><td>¹/₂</td><td>teaspoon salt</td></tr>
<tr><td>¹/₄</td><td>cup salad oil</td></tr>
<tr><td>3</td><td>egg yolks</td></tr>
<tr><td>¹/₄</td><td>cup water</td></tr>
<tr><td>1</td><td>teaspoon alcohol-free vanilla extract</td></tr>
<tr><td>3</td><td>egg whites</td></tr>
<tr><td>¹/₄</td><td>teaspoon cream of tartar</td></tr>
</table>

Each serving provides:
140 calories
2 g protein
6 g fat
20 g carbohydrate
160 mg sodium
53 mg cholesterol

1. Preheat oven to 325° F. oven (slow).
2. Sift together dry ingredients.
3. Add oil, egg yolks, water, and vanilla. Beat until very smooth.
4. Beat egg whites and cream of tartar until whites form very stiff peaks. Fold into egg yolk mixture.
5. Pour into ungreased 9" tube pan.
6. Bake 35 minutes or until firm to the touch. Invert pan to cool. Cool completely before removing from pan. 12 servings.

Variations:

COFFEE CHIFFON: Add 2 teaspoons instant coffee to dry ingredients.

LEMON CHIFFON: Substitute 1 teaspoon alcohol-free lemon extract for vanilla. Add 1 tablespoon fresh, grated lemon rind.

MAPLE CHIFFON: Substitute 1 teaspoon imitation maple flavoring for vanilla.

PEPPERMINT CHIFFON: Substitute 1 teaspoon peppermint flavoring for vanilla. Add a few drops of red food coloring.

(The American Dietetic Association's *Gluten Intolerance*)

CRISP 'N CHEWY COOKIES

Each serving provides:
95 calories
0 g protein
5 g total fat
13 g carbohydrate
89 mg sodium
0 mg cholesterol

$^1/_4$ cup salad oil
$^1/_2$ cup sugar
2   cups dry baby food rice cereal
2   teaspoons baking powder
1   jar (4 $^3/_4$ oz.) strained peaches
1   teaspoon alcohol-free almond extract

1. Preheat oven to 325° F. oven.
2. Grease baking sheet.
3. Combine all ingredients and stir lightly until mixture holds together.
4. Form dough into 1" balls. Press thin on baking sheet.
5. Bake 15 minutes. These cookies have crisp edges and chewy centers. 12 servings, 3 cookies each.

(The American Dietetic Association's *Gluten Intolerance*)

ORANGE SPONGE COOKIES

2	egg yolks
½	cup sugar
¼	teaspoon salt
1	teaspoon alcohol-free orange extract
½	cup potato starch flour
2	egg whites, stiffly beaten

Each serving provides:
50 calories
1 g protein
1 g fat
10 g carbohydrate
43 mg sodium
26 mg cholesterol

1. Preheat oven to 325° F. oven (slow).
2. Grease 8" square pan.
3. Beat egg yolks and sugar together until thick and lemon colored. Add salt, orange extract, and flour. Mix until smooth.
4. Fold in stiffly beaten egg whites. Pour into pan.
5. Bake 20 to 25 minutes until very lightly browned. Cool and cut into squares. 16 servings.

(The American Dietetic Association *Gluten Intolerance*)

Wheat-Free and Gluten-Free Cooking

☙ Special Products Recipes ❧

ENER-G MACARONI PASTA AND BEAN SOUP

Broth
Frozen green beans (approximately 1½ cups)
Water
1   can (15 oz.) pinto beans, rinsed, drained
1   package (10 oz.) frozen spinach
4   oz. Ener-G macaroni (¼ pkg. or 1½ cups)
1   clove minced garlic (optional)
Salt (optional)

1.   Place broth in pan and add green beans. Boil and then simmer until done, adding water if necessary. Add pinto beans.
2.   In a separate pan, cook spinach, drain and add to soup.
3.   Cook macaroni according to directions on package, rinse, drain, and add to soup.
4.   Heat thoroughly and serve.

To cook macaroni: Add 8 oz. (½ carton or 2 ¼ level cups) Ener-G Gluten-Free Macaroni to 2 ¾ quarts (11 cups) rapidly boiling water to which 1 tablespoon salt has been added (optional). Boil uncovered, stirring occasionally for 15 to 20 minutes or until tender but still firm. Drain and rinse with warm water.

(Ener-G Foods)

ENER-G SMALL SHELLS AND BEAN SOUP

2   cups cooked Ener-G Gluten-Free Small Shells
1   medium onion, chopped finely
1   large celery stalk, chopped finely
1   clove garlic, minced
2   tablespoons olive oil
2   cups water

$1/2$ cup tomato sauce
$2 1/2$ cups cooked small white beans
$1/4$ teaspoon salt
$1/8$ teaspoon pepper
$1/4$ teaspoon thyme
1   tablespoon chopped parsley

1. Cook Ener-G Gluten-Free Small Shells according to directions on package.
2. Saute the onion, celery, and garlic in oil until soft.
3. Add remaining ingredients except for small shells and simmer approximately 20 minutes. Stir occasionally.
4. Add Ener-G Gluten-Free Small Shells and additional water if necessary. Simmer for five minutes and serve.

To cook small shells: Add 8 oz. ($1/2$ carton) Ener-G Gluten-Free Small Shells to $2 3/4$ quarts of rapidly boiling water to which 1 teaspoon salt (optional) has been added. Boil uncovered, stirring occasionally for 10 to 15 minutes or until tender but still firm. Drain and rinse with warm water.

(Ener-G Foods)

ENER-G VERMICELLI TOMATO SOUP

2   onions, chopped fine
2   tablespoons oil
3   ripe sliced tomatoes
5   cups vegetable bouillon
1/4 teaspoon thyme
1   bay leaf
1/4 cup Ener-G Gluten-Free Vermicelli
1/4 teaspoon salt (optional)
     Pepper to taste

1.   Saute onions in oil. Reduce heat and add tomatoes. Stir and cook about 10 minutes.
2.   Add vegetable bouillon, thyme, and bay leaf.
3.   Cover and simmer for 15-20 minutes. Remove from heat and let cool. Remove bay leaf.
4.   Puree soup in blender. Return soup to pan and simmer briefly.
5.   Stir in cooked Ener-G Vermicelli (see below), salt, and pepper. Simmer for 10 minutes or until pasta is done.

To cook Vermicelli: Boil 1/2 package (8 oz.) Ener-G Gluten-free Vermicelli in 2 quarts water for 4 to 6 minutes. Drain and rinse with warm water.

(Ener-G Foods)

RICE BREAD FORMULA

1   package active dry yeast
$^7/_8$ cup water, divided
$1^1/_2$ cups rice flour (not brown rice flour)
1   teaspoon salt
2   tablespoons sugar
1   tablespoon Methocel (found in health food stores
      or may be obtained from Ener-G Foods)
1   tablespoon vegetable oil

1. Grease loaf pan (9 × 5 × 2 $^3/_4$) or muffin pan (12 cups).
2. Soak yeast in 1/4 cup warm water (105°-115° 115/f.) until dissolved (about 10 minutes).
3. Sift together flour, salt, sugar, and Methocel; set aside.
4. To small-size mixing bowl, add dissolved yeast, remaining warm water ($^5/_8$ cup), and oil. Gradually add $^2/_3$ of the dry ingredients to the liquid, mixing at slow speed. When ingredients are blended, increase to medium speed. Mix 5 minutes, scraping bowl and beaters occasionally. With mixer running, slowly add HALF of remaining flour mixture and beat well. Put mixer aside, add rest of dry ingredients and mix as well as possible by hand.
5. Dough will be quite stiff and sticky. Transfer dough to a piece of waxed paper, previously coated with

oil (about 1 tablespoon, enough to prevent dough from sticking onto paper) and mold the dough into loaf or rolls of desired size and shape, no larger than half the volume of baking pan. It helps to coat hands with oil.

6.   Let rise (proof) in warm, humid place for about 1 hour to 1½ hours until doubled in size, approximately to top of pan, but not much higher. (Do not overproof.) If quite warm, dough may rise in 30 minutes, or check occasionally. While dough is rising, preheat oven to 375°. Bake at 375° for 40 to 45 minutes for loaf or 30 to 35 minutes for rolls, until nicely browned. Remove from pan. Cool on rack.

(U.S.A. Rice Council)

LIST OF RESOURCES

Arrowhead Mills, Inc. P.O. Box 2059. Hereford, Texas 79045.

CPC International. *Recipes for People with Gluten Intolerance*. Coventry, CT: Best Foods, A Division of CPC International, Inc., 1992.

Dobler, Merri Lou, M.S., R.D. *Gluten Intolerance*. Chicago: The American Dietetic Association, 1991.

Eden Foods, Inc. "Healthy Recipes." Eden Foods, Inc. 701 Tecumseh Road. Clinton, Michigan 49236.

Ener-G Foods, Inc. "Recipes." Seattle: Ener-G Foods, Inc., 1993.

Frazier, Claude A., M.D. *Coping with Food Allergy*. New York: Times Books, 1974, revised 1985.

U.S.A. Rice Council. "Cooking with Rice." U.S.A. Rice Council. P.O. Box 740123, Houston, TX 77274.

———— . "Light, Lean, Low Fat." U.S.A. Rice Council. P.O. Box 740123, Houston, TX 77274.

———— . "Tasty Rice Recipes for Those with Allergies." U.S.A. Rice Council. P.O. Box 740123, Houston, TX 77274.

Vegetarian Resource Group. P.O. Box 1463. Baltimore, MD 29203.

Washington/Idaho Dry Pea and Lentil Commissions. 5071 Highway 8, West., Moscow, Idaho 83843.

CHAPTER TWO

Milk-Free and Lactose-Free Cooking

Everyone is supposed to drink two glasses of milk a day. Right? From babies to seniors, people are told they need the calcium and protein that two eight-ounce glasses of milk provide. Vegetarians especially have to worry about getting enough protein.

Yet intense discomfort can result from drinking a glass of milk if you are allergic or intolerant to its contents. A milk allergy will often follow an individual from infancy to adulthood and may be inherited.

Even if we avoid the recommended two glasses a day, milk or milk products may still turn up in many of our favorite foods. The main component of cheese and ice cream is, of course, milk. But lots of other dishes also contain milk: many bakery products, au gratin foods, biscuits, cream sauces and many gravies, cream soups, pasta products, many dried meat products which use dried milk as filler, puddings, etc.

Even if you are not allergic to milk, you may be lactose intolerant which means you lack the proper enzymes to digest cow's milk. Although most Americans have adapted genetically over time to cow's milk, there are still those who have not and must avoid the product entirely. A doctor can rule out this congenital problem in determining milk sensitivity.

Symptoms of milk allergy range from eczema and colic to diarrhea, croup, or asthma to even more diffuse symptoms of milk sensitivity. Symptoms of lactose intolerance may mimic those of cow's milk.

With the recognition of milk allergy or lactose intolerance comes the need to avoid milk and the products made from milk. So, how do we cook without milk? That chore is easier today than it was a few years ago because of all the substitutes in the market today. Many milk-free recipes call for substitutes such as infant formulas like ISOMIL or SOYALAC. Soy substitutes such as SOYALAC also comes in a formula that is corn-free and galactose-free (called I-SOYLAC). Other soy substitute products available in the marketplace today include: ProSobee and Sobee, MeadJohnson Company; Mull-soy and Neo-Mull-soy (no corn oil), Borden Company. Other recipes may call for non-dairy creamer as a substitute. A third substitute is made from rice. One such grain-based product on the market today is called Rice Dream.

Recipes calling for milk or cream are easily adapted to soy or rice substitutes. Cream sauces which are required in many soup and casserole recipes can be made according to the following directions for cream sauce, published by Nutricia, Inc.

BASIC CREAM SAUCE

	Thin	Medium	Thick
Vegetable margarine or oil	1 Tbsp	1 Tbsp	2 Tbsp
Thickening agent (use only one)			
Corn starch	1 Tbsp	2 Tbsp	3 Tbsp
Arrowroot flour	2 tsp	1½ Tbsp	2 Tbsp
Rice flour	2 tsp	1½ Tbsp	2 Tbsp
Salt	¼ tsp	¼ tsp	½ tsp
Soyalac or I-Soyalac	1 cup	1 cup	1 cup

To make the cream sauce with Soylac: Blend margarine or oil, one of the thickening agents, and salt. Then add Soyalac or I-Soyalac and water. Cook over low heat, stirring constantly until thick and thoroughly cooked. Use thin cream sauce for soups, medium for scalloped or creamed dishes and thick for croquettes.

(Nutricia, Inc.)

To make CREAM SAUCE WITH RICE DREAM:

2   tablespoons canola oil
5   tablespoons unbleached flour (can substitute 5 tablespoons of rice flour)
1   cup water or vegetable stock
1   cup Original Rice Dream
$^1/_2$ teaspoon sea salt
    Pinch white pepper

1. In a small saucepan, heat oil over medium heat. Add flour and gently stir for a few minutes.
2. Bring water or stock to a boil and slowly pour into flour/oil mixture; whisk vigorously.
3. Blend in Rice Dream, salt and pepper. Reduce flame to low or place a heat diffuser under the pan.
4. Cover and simmer for 10-15 minutes. Adjust seasonings to taste. Sauce will thicken as it cools and is best served immediately.
    Yield: 2 $^1/_2$ cups

Variations: For Indian cuisine, add 1 teaspoon curry powder; for an Italian flair, add $^1/_4$ teaspoon each of powdered garlic, dried basil and oregano; as a cream sauce for fish, add 1 teaspoon dried dill, 3 tablespoon lemon juice and 2 tablespoons capers.

(Imagine Foods)

Milk-Free and Lactose-Free Cooking

Pastries, Breads, and

Other Such Recipes

ORANGE MAPLE MACADAMIA BREAD

2	cups all-purpose flour (can substitute rice flour)	³/₄	cup maple syrup
1	teaspoon baking powder	¹/₂	cup buttermilk (can substitute soy or rice milk with 1 teaspoon of vinegar)
1	teaspoon baking soda		
¹/₈	teaspoon salt	¹/₄	cup Florida orange juice
1	large egg, lightly beaten	2	tablespoons grated orange zest
¹/₂	cup canola oil	5	ounces (1 cup) chopped macadamia nuts

1. Heat oven to 350° F. Grease and flour a 9 × 5 × 3-inch loaf pan.
2. Combine flour, baking powder, baking soda, and salt in medium bowl; set aside.
3. Whisk egg, butter, syrup, milk substitute and vinegar, Florida orange juice and orange zest in large bowl until blended. Beat in dry ingredients just until combined; fold in macadamia nuts. Pour into prepared pan.
4. Bake until toothpick inserted in center of loaf comes out clean, 45 to 50 minutes. Cool 5 minutes in pan on wire rack.
5. Turn bread onto wire rack, invert. Cool completely before serving.

(Florida Department of Citrus)

BROWN RICE-FLOUR PIE CRUST

$1^1/_2$ cups brown rice flour
$^1/_4$ cup potato flour
$^1/_2$ teaspoon salt
$^2/_3$ cup vegetable shortening
$^1/_2$ cup ice water
      Soy milk
      Sugar (optional)

1. Sift flours and salt together in a bowl.
2. Cut in shortening and blend well.
3. Add ice water a little at a time, blending thoroughly after each addition until dough forms a ball and leaves sides of bowl.
4. Roll out on waxed paper and place in pie plate. Brush top of pie crust with soy milk and sprinkle with sugar before baking (optional).
5. Bake at 425° F. for 10-15 minutes until golden brown.
    Yields double 9-inch pie crust.

(Allergy Information Association)

CREAMY HEARTY OATMEAL

2   cups Original Rice Dream
1   cup old fashioned rolled oats
1/4   cup raisins or chopped dates
        Pinch sea salt
1/4   teaspoon cinnamon (optional)
        Sprinkle of roasted nuts or seeds

1.   Place all ingredients in a saucepan. Bring to a boil.
2.   Cover (leaving lid ajar to prevent boiling over), reduce heat to very low and simmer for 10 minutes.
3.   Stir often. Serve topped with roasted nuts or seeds and fresh fruits of your choice.
     Yield: 2-3 servings.

(Imagine Foods)

Milk-Free and Lactose-Free Cooking

🌀 Main Dishes 🌀

GARDEN PIE

Make Brown Rice-Flour Pie Crust Recipe (see above)

4-5   cups assorted vegetables, chopped
      (corn, zucchini, tomatoes, cauliflower, peas, onion, mushrooms)
2   cups chopped tofu
¼   teaspoon sage
¼   teaspoon turmeric
¼   teaspoon cumin
¼   teaspoon salt
¼   teaspoon pepper
1-2   cups Basic Cream sauce

1.   Preheat oven to 350° F.
2.   Mix vegetables, white sauce, tofu, and spices.
3.   Place in crust and cover with top crust. Poke holes in top according to leaf design.
4.   Bake at 350° for about one hour.
     Yield one 9-inch pie.

TOFU-VEGETABLE STIR-FRY

2   tablespoons olive oil
1½   pound Tofu cut into ½-inch squares
¼   cup slivered almonds or whole cashews
3   stalks celery, finely sliced
1   onion, finely chopped
1   bell pepper, finely chopped
2   cups finely cut chinese cabbage
3   tablespoons arrowroot diluted with 1-2 Tbsp. water
1   teaspoon salt
       Light-sodium soy sauce to taste

1. Heat oil in a wok (or a heavy pan). Brown tofu well on all sides. Add nuts, brown, and set aside.
2. Stir fry celery and onion in wok until tender. Add other vegetable. Add a sprinkle of water.
3. When all vegetables are crispy tender, add diluted arrowroot and soy sauce.
4. Add tofu and nuts and serve immediately over rice.
    Yields 4 servings over rice.

FETTUCCINI PRIMAVERA WITH BECHAMEL SAUCE

3   tablespoons extra virgin olive oil
2   cloves garlic, minced
1   head broccoli, thinly cut
1   large red pepper, thinly sliced
10   large mushrooms, thinly sliced
1   small red onion, sliced
1   cup frozen baby peas, thawed

$1/2$ cup fresh basil, cut into strips
$1/2$ cup black olives, sliced
12   oz. fettuccini pasta (gluten-free available)
3   cups Bechamel sauce (see Soups, Sauces, and Gravies in Chapter Two)
Garnish with basil flowers

1. In a medium pan, saute broccoli and garlic in olive oil for 5 minutes.
2. Add peppers and mushrooms; saute over medium heat for 5-10 minutes more, depending upon how well cooked you prefer your vegetables.
3. Stir in peas; cook a few more minutes until mixture is hot. Add olives and basil; cover and set aside.
4. Cook non-gluten pasta following package directions. Serve immediately topped with sauteed vegetable us portion of Bechamel sauce. Garnish with basil flowers.
   Yield: 4-6 servings.

(Imagine Foods)

TAMALE PIE

Prep. Time: 15 minutes
Cooking Time: 40 minutes

Filling:

2	tablespoons Eden Hot Pepper Sesame Oil
1	medium onion, chopped
1	clove garlic, pressed
$1/2$	cup fresh or frozen corn
$1/2$	cup green pepper, chopped
$1/2$	cup black or green olives, chopped
2	15 oz. cans Eden Organic Pinto, Black or Kidney Beans, drained
1	cup Eden Organic Spaghetti Sauce
$1/2$	teaspoon cumin
$1/2$-1	teaspoon chili powder

1. Heat oil; saute onions and garlic.
2. Add remaining ingredients and saute briefly, and set aside.
3. Prepare topping.

Topping:

²/₃ cup Eden Yellow Cornmeal
²/₃ cup organic whole wheat flour
(or ²/₃ cup rice flour)
1 teaspoon aluminum-free baking powder
¹/₂ teaspoon sea salt
³/₄ cup Edensoy Original Organic
3 tablespoons Eden Olive Oil
2 tablespoons Eden Organic Barley Malt or
Honey (use honey in gluten intolerant)

1. Sift dry ingredients together.
2. In a separate bowl, mix liquids.
3. Combine wet and dry.
4. Place filling in oiled deep dish pie plate.
5. Pour cornmeal topping gently over the top.
6. Bake at 350° F. for 40 minutes.
Yields: 6-8 servings.

(Eden Foods)

Milk-Free and Lactose-Free Cooking

❧ Side Dishes ☙

CREAMED BROCCOLI

2   cups broccoli cut into small pieces
2   tablespoons chopped parsley
1   cup medium cream sauce (see recipe
      for Basic Cream Sauce)

1.   Mix cream sauce and broccoli and heat thoroughly.
2.   Garnish with chopped parsley.

Variation: Any other desired vegetable may be used in place of broccoli.

(Nutricia, Inc.)

CITRUS SALAD WITH BIBB LETTUCE, WATERCRESS AND BALSAMIC DRESSING

Each serving provides:
126 calories
2 g protein
23 g carbohydrate
4 g fat
0 mg cholesterol
145 mg sodium
4.7 g fiber
103 mg Vitamin C

1   medium pink grapefruit, peeled, pith removed, and cut into sections
2   large oranges, peeled, pith removed, and cut into sections
2   tangerines, peeled and separated into sections
1   bunch watercress leaves, rinsed and patted dry
3   tablespoons orange juice
1   tablespoons balsamic vinegar, or to taste
¼   teaspoon salt
1   tablespoon canola or other vegetable oil
1   large head of Bibb lettuce, separated into leaves, rinsed and patted dry
    Peel from one orange, cut into very fine julienne strips.
1. In a medium bowl, combine the grapefurit, oranges, tangerines, and watercress.

2. In a small bowl, combine the orange juice, Balsamic vinegar, and salt. Add the oil and whisk the dressing until it is combined. Pour over the fruit and watercress and gently toss to combine.
3. Line four serving plates with the Bibb lettuce. Divide the fruit mixture among the plates and garnish each with the julienned orange peel.
   Yields four servings.

(Florida Department of Citrus)

Milk-Free and Lactose-Free Cooking

◖ Soups, Sauces, and Gravies ◗

RICE DREAM BECHAMEL SAUCE

4 tablespoons butter, ghee, or olive oil
1 small yellow onion, finely chopped
1 clove garlic, minced
6 tablespoons whole wheat or brown rice flour
Optional splash of white wine or lemon

1 cup Original Rice Dream
$\frac{1}{2}$ cup water or vegetable stock
Pinch dried dill
$\frac{1}{2}$ teaspoon sea salt
Pinch white pepper

1. In a heavy saucepan, over a low flame, saute onions and garlic in butter/oil until soft and translucent.
2. Sprinkle in flour and stir frequently for 5 minutes. Slowly add Rice Dream, water/stock and seasonings. Whisk until well blended.
3. Increase heat and allow the mixture to come briefly to a boil. Reduce heat to low and simmer for 5 minutes, stirring often.
4. Taste, adjust seasonings and/or sauce thickness by adding more water or flour in small increments.
5. Serve immediately or allow to cool and refrigerate for later use.
   Yield: 2 cups.

Variations: For a different flavor or texture, add a small amount of chopped fresh spinach, chives, scallions, roasted peppers, 1 tablespoon of capers or a touch of toasted sesame oil.

(Imagine Foods)

SPLIT PEA SOUP

2   cups split peas
4   cups of water
1-2 tablespoons olive oil
2   carrots, diced
2   stalks of celery, diced
1   onion, diced
1   teaspoon celery salt

1. Combine above ingredients in a large sauce pan and cook until tender (about 45 minutes).
2. Puree in blender until smooth and serve.
   Yields: 4 servings.

VEGETABLE CHOWDER

1	tablespoon oleic safflower or canola oil
1	small onion, diced
1	large celery stalk, thinly sliced
1	large carrot, thinly sliced
1	clove garlic, finely diced
2	cups water
1	medium russet potato, peeled & diced

2	ripe tomatoes, chopped
1/2	cup fresh or frozen corn
2	tablespoons tamari soy sauce
1	teaspoon basil
1	large bay leaf
1/2	teaspoon sea salt
	Pinch black pepper
2	cups Original Rice Dream

1. In a 3-quart saucepan, saute onions in oil until translucent.
2. Add celery, carrots, and garlic; saute for several more minutes.
3. Add water, potatoes, corn, and seasonings, bring to a boil and then reduce heat to a simmer. Cover and cook for 15 minutes.
4. Add tomatoes and simmer for 15 minutes longer. Add Rice Dream and adjust seasonings, to taste. Yield: 5-6 servings.

(Imagine Foods)

BLUEBERRY ORANGE SAUCE

$^1/_2$ cup fresh or thawed frozen blueberries
$^1/_4$ cup Florida orange juice concentrate
1   tablespoon sugar
1   teaspoon grated orange zest
$^1/_2$ cup Florida fresh orange sections, cut into bite-size pieces

Each serving (3 Tbsp.) provides:
66 calories
1 g protein
16 g carbohydrate
.8 g dietary fiber
0 g fat
0 mg cholesterol
2 mg sodium

1. In a medium saucepan, heat all the ingredients over medium heat, stirring frequently until thick and syrupy, five to seven minutes.
2. Serve over pancakes or crepes.
   Yields: $1^1/_4$ cups.

(Florida Department of Citrus)

HERBED GRAVY

¹/₃   cup whole wheat pastry flour (may substitute non-gluten flour, see Chapter Two)
1   cup Original Rice Dream
1   tablespoon soy sauce
1   cup water
¹/₂   teaspoon sea salt
2   tablespoons oleic safflower or canola oil
1   teaspoon dried, crushed sage
¹/₄   teaspoon thyme
¹/₄   teaspoon marjoram
       Pinch black pepper

1.   In a 2-quart saucepan, heat oil over medium heat. Add flour, and stir often for two minutes.
2.   Remove from heat and allow to cool for several minutes.
3.   In a separate bowl, combine remaining ingredients. Whisk together with the flour/oil, half at a time to avoid lumping.
4.   Bring to boil over medium heat, stirring often. Reduce heat to low and cook for 10-15 minutes, stirring occasionally.

5. If gravy seems too thick, simply whisk in additional water, 1 tablespoon at a time until desired consistency reached.
6. Adjust salt and pepper to taste. Gravy will thicken as it cools.
    Yields: 1¹/₂ or 2 cups.

Note: Stores well in the refrigerator for several days. To serve at a later time, reheat slowly over a medium flame, making sure to stir well. Add a tablespoon or two of water if necessary.

Variations: For a delicious Mushroom Gravy: add sauteed mushrooms and onions when gravy is simmering. Eliminate herbs and adjust other seasonings to taste.

(Imagine Foods)

GREEN GODDESS DRESSING

1	medium green onion (scallion)
1	medium clove garlic
4	sprigs parsley
³/₄	teaspoon sea salt
3	tablespoons tahini
1	cup Original Rice Dream
1	tablespoon umeboshi plum paste or plums
¹/₃	cup canola or oleic safflower oil

1. Combine all ingredients in blender or food processor; blend until smooth.
2. Adjust seasonings to taste.
   Yields: 6 servings or 1¹/₂ cups.

(Imagine Foods)

Milk-Free and Lactose-Free Cooking

❧ Desserts ❧

OATMEAL COOKIES

³/₄ cup vegetable shortening
1 cup firmly packed brown sugar
¹/₂ cup granulated sugar
1 large egg
¹/₃ cup soy milk
1 teaspoon vanilla

3 cups plus 1 Tbsp. oats, uncooked
1 cup all-purpose flour
1 teaspoon salt
¹/₂ teaspoon cinnamon
¹/₂ teaspoon baking soda

1. Preheat oven to 350°.
2. Beat together shortening, sugar, egg, soy milk, and vanilla until creamy.
3. Add combined remaining ingredients. Mix well until blended.
4. Drop by rounded teaspoonfuls onto greased cookie sheet.
5. Bake at 350° for 12 minutes.

Variation: Add raisins, coconut, or chopped dates.

(Nutricia, Inc.)

FUDGE BROWNIES (OR CAROB)

¹/₂	cup soy margarine
2	squares (2 oz.) unsweetened chocolate (2 oz. of carob may be substituted if chocolate is not tolerated)
1	cup sugar
¹/₂	cup wheat or rice flour
¹/₂	teaspoon baking powder
¹/₂	teaspoon salt
2	eggs
1	teaspoon vanilla
¹/₂	cup chopped nuts

1. Preheat oven to 325°, and grease an 8-inch square pan.
2. Melt margarine and chocolate over low heat.
3. Sift together dry ingredients and stir into chocolate mixture; cool slightly.
4. Add eggs, vanilla, and nuts. Beat until smooth. Pour into pan.
5. Bake 20 to 25 minutes. Don't over bake. Cool and cut into squares.
   Yields 16 brownies.

(ROSS General Information Series: Food Sensitivity)

GRAPEFRUIT SORBET WITH CANDIED ZEST (Need Ice Cream Freezer)

3-4	large Florida grapefruit
2	cups sugar
1	cup water
2	tablespoons lime juice

> **Each serving provides:**
> 205 calories
> 1 g protein
> 55 g carbohydrate
> 0.1 g dietary fiber
> 0 g fat
> 0 mg cholesterol
> 1 mg sodium
> 114 mg potassium
> 32 mg Vitamin C

1. Grate enough grapefruit zest (rind) to make ½ cup; set aside.
2. Juice grapefruit to make 2 cups juice. Strain juice to remove any seeds, reserving pulp and combining with juice.
3. In a 1-quart saucepan, combine sugar, water and zest and bring to a boil over medium-high heat. Remove from heat and remove 3/4 of the zest with a slotted spoon and allow to cool.
4. Set aside the zest in a covered container and refrigerate until the sorbet is ready to serve. Combine the cooled syrup with the grapefruit juice and lime juice and refrigerate until cold.
5. Place mixture in an ice cream freezer and freeze according to manufacturer's directions.
6. Transfer sorbet to a 1-quart plastic container. Cover with plastic wrap (to prevent ice crystals) and plastic lid. Place in freezer until ready to serve. Allow to stand 10 minutes before scooping. Garnish each serving with reserved candied zest, mint leaf, and additional grapefruit points if desired. Yields about 1 quart or 8 servings.

(Florida Department of Citrus)

LIST OF REFERENCES

Allergy Information Association. *The Allergy Cookbook: Diets Unlimited for Limited Diets.* Methuen: New York, 1983.

Eden Foods, Inc. 701 Tecumseh Road, Clinton, MI 49236.

Florida Department of Citrus. Lakeland, Florida 33802-0148.

Imagine Foods, 350 Cambridge Avenue, Suite 350, Palo Alto, CA 94306.

Nutricia, Inc. "Milk-Free Recipes Using Soyalac and I-Soyalac." Nutricia, Inc., 11503 Pierce Street, Riverside, CA 92505.

Ross General Information Series. "Food Sensitivity." Abbott Ross Laboratories, P.O. Box 500010. El Paso, TX 88550-0010.

CHAPTER THREE

Milk-Free, Egg-Free, Wheat-Free, and Gluten-Free Cooking

So, why clump these different allergies together in a group? It is because these four are among the most prevalent of the food allergies and are frequently found jointly affecting an individual. Allergic reactions to this food combination can take place in almost any bodily system: gastrointestinal, respiratory, cutaneous (skin), urinary, nervous, mucous, gland, membrances, and even the circulatory system if the reaction is severe and moves into anaphylactic shock. Gastrointestinal disorder is, however, the most common reaction.

Sensitivity to food alone may be the sole cause of the symptoms experienced, but this is less common than sensitivity to several allergies. For example, some allergic persons react to milk at any time; others react only during pollen season.

A person so affected must plan their diet to avoid this combination of food and sometimes others. The question arises: Is there anything left to eat after we omit milk, eggs, wheat, and gluten products from a vegetarian diet, especially if a person may also be allergic to other foods such as peanuts or soybeans and need to avoid those as well?

Sometimes a person may tolerate, without symptoms, several foods when eaten separately but may suffer a severe reaction if the foods are combined at one meal, say in a casserole. Consequently, we are back to looking for recipes that allow us to cook delicious meals without this combination of food allergens and any other we may be sensitive to. We have included recipes for each part of the meal which omit or use substitutes for these four common allergens. You can use substitutions given in earlier chapters to transform old-favorites among your own recipes.

Milk-Free, Egg-Free, Wheat-Free, and Gluten-Free Cooking

Pastries, Breads, and

Other Such Recipes

PANCAKES

1³/₄   SOYALAC/I-SOYALAC
3   tablespoons vegetable oil
1   cup sifted rice flour
2   tablespoons cornstarch
2   tablespoons sugar or molasses
¹/₂   teaspoon salt
1¹/₄ teaspoon baking powder

1.   Combine liquid ingredients, then blend dry ingredients. Pour liquid ingredients into the dry mixture and stir until mixture is smooth.
2.   Bake on preheated griddle in small cakes or until each pancake is full of bubbles and the undersurface is brown. Turn and brown on other side. Serve while hot with any syrup or sweet that is allowed, such as blueberry-orange sauce.

(Nutricia, Inc.)

RYE BAKING POWDER BISCUITS

2   cups rye flour
1   tablespoon baking powder
$^1/_4$ teaspoon salt
$^1/_4$ cup shortening
$^1/_4$ cup water

1. Sift together dry ingredients, then cut in the shortening until dough texture is like coarse cornmeal. Stir in the water with a fork.
2. Roll out to $^1/_2$" thickness on a lightly floured board. Cut and bake on a greased cookie sheet for 12-15 minutes at 450° F.

(Margaret L. Williams' *Cooking Without*)

RICE-APRICOT MUFFINS

1¹/₂   cups rice flour
1   tablespoon baking powder
1   tablespoon sugar
2   tablespoons oil
³/₄   cup apricot nectar

1. Combine dry ingredients. Stir in oil and juice.
2. Form into patties and place in greased or lined tins. Set aside for ten minutes.
3. Bake at 400° F. for 25 minutes.

(Margaret L. Williams' *Cooking Without*)

POTATO RYE BURGER BUNS

2   package dry yeast
3/4   cup warm water
1   tablespoon sugar
3   cups rye flour
1^1/$_2$ cups cold mashed potatoes (instant okay)
2   teaspoons salt
2   tablespoons oil

1. Dissolve yeast and sugar in water and let stand for 10 minutes.
2. Add other ingredients and blend thoroughly. Knead 5 or 6 minutes and cover in a bowl to rise about 1^1/$_2$ hours.
3. Knead one more minute and divide into ^{1}/$_2$ cup round mound and place into 2^1/$_2$" foil baking cups, greased. Let rise 20 minutes.
4. Bake 15-20 minutes at 350° F. oven.

(Margaret L. Williams' *Cooking Without*)

BOSTON BROWN BREAD

1	cup cornmeal
1	cup rye flour
$7/8$	cup rice flour
$1/2$	teaspoon salt
2	teaspoons soda
$3/4$	cup molasses
$1^1/3$	cup soy milk
1	teaspoon vinegar
$3/4$	cup raisins
$1/2$	cup chopped walnuts
1	tablespoon finely grated orange rind

1. Mix together the cornmeal, rye flour, rice flour, salt, and soda.
2. Mix the molasses, soy milk, and vinegar together and add to mixture.
3. Add raisins, nuts, and orange rind. Mix everything together well.
4. Pour into a well-greased can or mold, $2/3$ full. Cover tightly. Place the mold in a pan with one inch of boiling water. Place in a 350° F. oven and steam for 3 hours, replacing the water as it evaporates.
5. Cool and remove from mold. Yields: one loaf.

Milk-Free, Egg-Free, Wheat-Free, and Gluten-Free Cooking

◖ Main Dishes ◗

PASTA WITH SUNFLOWER KERNELS

8	oz. tomato, spinach pasta (wheat-free/gluten free variety)
3	Parsley springs, chopped
3	garlic cloves, minced
1	teaspoon grated lemon peel
1/2	cup sunflower oil
1/2	teaspoon each salt and pepper
2/3	cup grated Parmesan cheese
1/2	cup toasted sunflower kernels

1. Cook pasta according to package directions; drain.
2. In a small skillet, heat parsley, garlic, and lemon peel in oil one minute. Add salt and pepper.
3. Pour over pasta, add Parmesan cheese and sunflower kernels. Toss lightly.
   Makes 4 servings.

(National Sunflower Association)

GOOD GRAIN BURGERS

1	onion, minced
1	carrot, grated
1	stalk celery, minced
2	tablespoons fresh parsley, minced
2	tablespoons sesame seeds or sunflower seeds
1	tablespoon olive oil
3	cups cooked, cooled grains
1	tablespoon soy flour
1/2	cup nut butter
	Salt and pepper to taste

1. Saute the onion, carrot, celery, and parsley in the butter or oil until tender.
2. Mix all the ingredients together. Adjust the amounts of nut butter and soy flour used according the texture of the grain chosen in order to shape mixture into patties. Season to taste.
3. Fry in olive oil until golden brown. Serve on non-gluten rolls (see pastry section) or serve with nut gravy (see soup/sauce sections). Makes 10 to 12 burgers.

Variation: Substitute lentils or pureed beans for part of the cooked grains.

BOSTON BAKED BEANS

2	cups navy beans or soy beans	2	tablespoons olive oil
1	large onion, chopped	1/2	teaspoon salt
3	medium tomatoes, pureed	1/4	teaspoon cloves
1/2	cup molasses	1/2	teaspoon dry mustard
1/2	cup dark brown sugar, packed		

1. Soak beans overnight. Then rinse and drain.
2. Place beans, onion, and oil in a pot with water to cover and bring to a boil. Pour into baking dish, making sure that liquid covers the beans.
3. Mix and add remaining ingredients and stir.
4. Cover and bake for 5 hours in a 350° F. oven, checking every hour or so and replenishing the water so that it continually covers the beans.
5. After 5 hours, remove the lid. Add water to cover the beans once more, and bake uncovered for 1 to 1½ hours, until a little liquid remains as a thick sauce and the beans are a rich brown color. Yields six servings.

BLACK-EYED PEA PANCAKES

1	cup dry black eye peas
3	cups water for soaking
¼	teaspoon cardamon
¼	teaspoon ginger
¼	teaspoon turmeric
¼	teaspoon salt
¼	teaspoon black pepper
2	tablespoons olive oil

1. Soak black-eyed peas overnight or 7-8 hours.
2. Grind small batches of black-eyed peas in blender, doing a small amount at a time.
3. Add water until you have thick pancake batter consistency.
4. Add spices.
5. Heat olive oil in skillet and drop approximately ⅛ cup of batter into heated oil. Fry until golden brown on both sides.

FALAFEL

Prep. Time: 30 minutes
Cooking Time: 10 minutes

$^1/_2$ cup millet, cooked in 1$^1/_2$ cups water (30-40 minutes)
1 tablespoon Eden Olive Oil
3 cloves garlic, pressed
1 medium onion, chopped
1 15 oz. can Eden Organic Garbanzo Beans, drained
2 tablespoons sesame tahini
2 tablespoons lemon juice
2 tablespoons parsley, chopped
2 teaspoons cumin
$^1/_2$ teaspoon sea salt
$^1/_4$ teaspoon cayenne pepper
1 tablespoon organic whole wheat flour (see wheat substitute in Chapter Two)
$^1/_2$ cup organic cornmeal

1. Cook millet and set aside.
2. Heat oil; saute garlic and onion.
3. Blend garbanzo beans in a food processor with tahini and lemon.
4. In a bowl, mix together all the ingredients except the cornmeal.

5. Shape into patties or croquettes and coat with cornmeal. Fry in hot oil and serve with sauce.
    Yield: 6 patties, 15-19 croquettes.

SAUCE

$^1/_2$ cup Edensoy Original Organic
1 tablespoon sesame tahini
$^1/_2$ teaspoon cumin
1-2 tablespoons lemon juice
2 cloves garlic, pressed

Combine all ingredients in a blender or food processor.
Yield: $^2/_3$ cup sauce.

(Eden Foods)

Milk-Free, Egg-Free, Wheat-Free, and Gluten-Free Cooking

⟪ Side Dishes ⟫

CARROT RICE CASSEROLE

3	cups cooked sliced carrots— save ³/₄ cup cooking liquid		2	tablespoons rice flour
2	cups cooked rice		1	teaspoon seasoned salt
¹/₄	cup finely chopped onion		¹/₄	teaspoon pepper
2	ounce jar chopped pimento, drained		1	teaspoon dill weed
1	cup SOYALAC OR I-SOYALAC		1	teaspoon salt

1. Preheat oven to 350° F.
2. Drain carrots, saving ³/₄ cup cooking liquid. Place sliced carrots into 2-quart casserole with rice, parsley, onion, and pimento.
3. Heat SOYALAC/I-SOYALAC slightly and gradually stir in 2 tablespoons rice flour. Continue to heat until slightly thick. Remove from heat and mix carrot liquid seasoning into SOYALAC/I-SOYALAC mixture. Pour liquid mixture over vegetables in casserole and mix lightly. Sprinkle with paprika. Bake for 20 minutes.

(Nutricia, Inc.)

HERBED WALNUT RICE

$1/2$	cup chopped onion
$1/2$	cup shredded carrot
$1/2$	cup walnuts, chopped
$1/4$	teaspoon dried marjoram
$1/4$	teaspoon dried thyme leaves
$1/8$	teaspoon dried rosemary
1	tablespoon butter or olive oil
3	cups cooked rice (cooked in chicken or vegetable broth)
2	tablespoons chopped fresh parsley

Each serving provides:
199 calories
6.9 g protein
23 g carbohydrate
9.1 g fat
1.2 g dietary fiber
6 mg cholesterol
549 mg sodium

1. Cook onion, carrot, walnuts, marjoram, thyme, and rosemary in butter/oil in large skillet over medium-high heat until vegetables are tender crisp.
2. Stir in rice and parsley; heat thoroughly.
   Makes 6 servings.

(U.S.A. Rice Council)

ROASTED POTATOES WITH HERBS

2	pounds boiling potatoes, about 6 or 7
4	bay leaves or rosemary
3	tablespoons olive oil
1	teaspoon salt
¼	teaspoon pepper

1. Heat the oven to 375° F. Break the bay leaves into pieces and put in a roasting pan with the oil, 1 teaspoon salt and ¼ teaspoon pepper. Put the pan in the oven enough to heat the oil.
2. Peel the potatoes and cut them into chunks. Toss the potatoes with oil to coat.
3. Cover the pan tightly with foil and bake 30 minutes. Remove the foil and continue baking, stirring occasionally, until the potatoes are crisp and well-browned, about thirty minutes longer.

HERBED GREEN BEANS WITH SUNFLOWER SEEDS

1   pound fresh green beans
2   cups water
1/2   teaspoon basil
1/2   teaspoon marjoram
1   tablespoon parsley
1/4   teaspoon thyme
1   small onion, chopped
1   clove garlic, minced
2   tablespoons olive oil
1/2   cup sunflower seeds
1   teaspoon salt
1/4   teaspoon freshly ground black pepper

1.   Wash beans, drain, snap and string. Steam until done.
2.   Combine herbs in bowl and set aside.
3.   Saute onion and garlic in olive oil and add herb mixture and seeds.
4.   Add beans and toss in skillet until thoroughly mixed.

Milk-Free, Egg-Free, Wheat-Free, and Gluten-Free Cooking

✿ Soups, Sauces, and Gravies ✿

NUT GRAVY

2   tablespoons butter or olive oil
2   tablespoons soy flour plus 1 Tbsp potato starch flour
2   cups soy milk
1   cup ground roasted almonds or cashews
1/2 teaspoon salt

1.   Heat oil in a skillet. Add flour and stir for one minute.
2.   Add soy milk and stir to prevent lumps. Add ground nuts.
3.   Heat to a simmer, stirring constantly until thickened. Salt.
     Makes three cups.

VEGETABLE SOUP

2	tablespoons olive oil
5	cups chopped vegetables (may use onion, celery, cabbage, squash, okra, carrots, peas, green beans, potatoes)
$1/4$	teaspoon rosemary
$1/4$	teaspoon basil
1	bay leaf
1	can Italian seasoned stewed tomatoes
1	can Spanish seasoned stewed tomatoes
1	can other stewed tomatoes
	Salt and pepper to taste

1. Saute vegetables in olive oil for five minutes.
2. Add stewed tomatoes and herbs.
3. Cover and simmer for 1 or 2 hours.
4. Remove bay leaf and season with salt and pepper.
   Yields about 8 cups.

CREAMED TOMATO SOUP

2   cups ripe tomatoes, chopped
1   cup water or vegetable broth
2   cups Basic Cream Sauce (see above)
      Salt and pepper to taste

1. Puree the tomatoes with the water or broth in a blender.
2. Pour in sauce pan and simmer, covered, for 20 minutes.
3. Slowly stir in Basic Cream Sauce, stirring constantly.
4. Season to taste and garnish with minced parsley.
   Yields 5 cups.

MEATLESS SPAGHETTI SAUCE

¹/₂	cup olive oil
¹/₂	pound onions peeled and sliced
2	zucchini, about ¹/₂ lb. total, sliced
3	garlic cloves
¹/₂	cup mushrooms, sliced
10	parsley sprigs, leaves only
1	teaspoon salt

¹/₂	teaspoon black pepper
2	medium-sized green peppers, chopped
1¹/₂	canned, peeled plum tomatoes, chopped and sieved
2	large ripe tomatoes, chopped fine
2	tablespoons tomato sauce, heaping

1. Heat olive oil in a skillet. Add onions and mushrooms and brown slowly for 10 minutes.
2. Chop garlic and parsley together and add to onions along with salt and pepper. Cover and cook for 10 minutes.
3. Add green pepper and zucchini and cook for 5 minutes.
4. Add canned and fresh tomatoes and cook slowly for 40 minutes.
5. Add tomato paste, stir well and remove from heat. Add more salt if necessary.
   Makes 4 cups. Serve over wheat-free/gluten-free pasta.

Milk-Free, Egg-Free, Wheat-Free, and Gluten-Free Cooking

◖ Desserts ◗

CHOCOLATE FRUIT CRISPIES

6	cups crisp rice cereal
¹/₂	cup raisins
¹/₂	cup finely chopped dried apricots
1	bag (10 oz.) large marshmallows
¹/₂	cup (3 oz.) semisweet chocolate morsels
2	tablespoons soy or rice milk
	Vegetable Cooking Spray

Each crispy provides:
25 calories
0.3 g protein
0.3 g fat
5.5 g carbohydrate
0.1 g dietary fiber
24 mg sodium
0 mg cholesterol

1. Combine cereal, raisins, and apricots in large bowl; set aside.
2. Combine marshmallows, chocolate, and milk in 2-quart saucepan. Place over low heat and cook, stirring about 10 minutes or until melted. Pour over cereal mixture; mix well.
3. Coat 12 × 8 × 2 inch baking pan with cooking spray; spread mixture evenly into pan. Press down firmly using fingers coated with cooking spray. Cover and chill until firm. Cut into one-inch squares.

Microwave Instructions:
1. Combine cereal, raisins, and apricots in large bowl; set aside.
2. Combine marshmallows, chocolate, and milk in 1¹/₂-quart microproof dish. Cook uncovered on HIGH 1 minute; stir until smooth. Continues as directed above. Makes 8 dozen crispies.

(U.S.A. Rice Council)

RICE-APPLE CRISP

2	cups cooked rice
1	can (20 oz.) pie-sliced apples
1	tablespoon lemon juice
1	cup brown sugar, divided
$^1/_2$	teaspoon ground cinnamon
$^1/_4$	teaspoon salt
$^3/_4$	cup rice flour
6	tablespoon milk-free margarine
$^1/_2$	cup chopped nut meats

1. Combine, rice, apples, lemon juice, $^1/_2$ cup sugar, cinnamon, and salt in greased shallow baking dish.
2. Mix rice flour and remaining sugar. Cut in margarine until mixture is crumbly. Stir in nut meats. Sprinkle over rice-apple mixture.
3. Bake at 350° F. oven for 30 minutes. Serve warm topped with whipped cream, if desired.
   Yields: 6 servings.

(U.S.A. Rice Council)

FRUIT COOKIES

½ cup milk-free margarine
1½ cups brown sugar, firmly packed
1 portion egg substitute
2 cups sifted rice flour
1 teaspoon baking soda
½ teaspoon salt

1 teaspoon ground cinnamon
1 teaspoon ground cloves
½ teaspoon ground nutmeg
1 cup finely grated apple
1 cup raisins
1 cup chopped nut meats
¼ cup milk substitute

1. Cream margarine and sugar together until fluffy.
2. Add egg substitute and continue beating until light and fluffy.
3. Sift together flour, soda, salt, cinnamon, cloves, and nutmeg. Stir in half the dry mixture and blend.
4. Add the apples, raisins, nuts, and milk substitute. Stir in remaining dry mixture and mix well.
5. Drop by teaspoon onto greased cookie sheet and bake at 350° F. oven for 10 to 15 minutes. Yields: about 6 dozen cookies.

(U.S.A. Rice Council)

LORI'S EASY PUMPKIN PIE

1   cup Original or Vanilla Rice Dream
2   portions egg substitute
2   cups unsweetened canned pumpkin (16 oz. can)
1/2   cup maple syrup
1   teaspoon cinnamon
1/2   teaspoon ground ginger
1/2   teaspoon nutmeg
1/2   teaspoon allspice
1/2   teaspoon sea salt
1   unbaked 9-inch pie crust (see Chapter Two)

1. Pre-heat oven to 425° F.
2. Mix all ingredients and pour into unbaked pie shell.
3. Bake for 15 minutes, reduce heat to 350° and bake for 40-50 minutes, or until inserted knife comes out clean.
4. Remove from oven and set on a wire rack to cool.
    Yields: 9-inch pie.

(Imagine Foods)

LIST OF REFERENCES

Eden Foods, Inc. 701 Tecumseh Road. Clinton, MI 49236.

Imagine Foods. "Rice Dream Natural Recipes." Imagine Foods. 350 CambridgeAvenue. Suite 350. Palo Alto, CA 94306.

National Sunflower Agency. 4023 State Street, Bismarck, N.D. 58501.

Nutricia, Inc. 11503 Pierce St., Riverside, CA 93505

USA Rice Council. P.O. Box 740123, Houston, TX 77274.

Williams, Margaret L. *Cooking Without: Recipes for the Allergic Child (and Family)*. Ambler, PA: The Gimbal Corporation, 1981.